LIFE ON THE TYNE

Daniel M Turner

White Wings
PUBLISHING

First published October 2016 by White Wings Publishing,
North Shields, Tyne and Wear, England

www.whitewingspublishing.co.uk

ISBN 978-0-9930205-2-0

Victor Noble Rainbird paintings included by courtesy of
David Hirst and Dave Young

Cuddy (Male Eider) Duck design © Cathy McCracken

Designed and typeset by Raspberry Creative Type,
Edinburgh

Printed by Elanders Ltd,
Merlin Way, New York Business Park, North Tyneside
NE27 0QG

DEDICATION

For everyone who has sailed upon the Tyne,
dipped in their toes,
watched the ripples and the tide's ebb and flow,
heard the lapping water and cries of gulls, tasted salty air
… things so dear, of home and northern life,

… and for those who have yet to come … to Tyneside,
don't wait too long.

Tyne dawn with Collingwood's monument, 28 July 2016 : (Ref 0327) EOS 7D Mk II; EFS 17-85 mm lens; focal length 85 mm;
f/14; 1/800 sec; ISO-1000

DOROTHY D

Fishing boat *Dorothy D* (ME 45; registered in Montrose) sailing up the Tyne to North Shields fish quay. For another photograph of *Dorothy D* see page 54.

Returning to the fish quay, 17 July 1986 :
(Ref 151-04) Chinon 135 mm lens with Y2 filter;
Kodak Tri-X; f/8 ½; 1/250 sec

CONTENTS

A wild salmon caught near the river mouth, August 2016

RED ARROWS OVER THE TYNE

The Red Arrows RAF display team performed over South Shields, Tynemouth and North Shields at the end of the Great North Run. Here we see two of the BAE Systems Hawk T1 jets tearing north and two dashing south towards Marsden. In the foreground is long, wooden Lloyds jetty (see also pages 15 and 30) and the red lighthouse (first lit in 1882) on Herd Groyne in South Shields. This Sunday brought the 36th Great North Run – an annual half marathon starting in Newcastle and finishing on the sea front at South Shields. Many of the runners are sponsored by their friends to raise funds for charities. Today, British runner Mo Farah won the elite men's race (in 1 hour 0 mins and 4 seconds) for the third time in a row while Kenyan athlete Vivian Cheruiyot won the elite women's race in 1:07.54. The day brought 57,000 participants ... spectators watched with delight.

At the river mouth, 11 September 2016 : (Photo Ref 1698) EOS 7D Mk II; EFS 17-85 mm lens; focal length 59 mm; f/14; 1/1000 sec; ISO-400

FOREWORD

I have visited the banks of the Tyne all my life. Our magnificent river flows endlessly; its upper reaches of freshwater merge into saltiness during its descent. The Tyne brings life to our region and its reach is global – with a rich ship building heritage and visiting vessels travelling from every corner of the world. River industry continues, reduced from the past, but ferries still ply to and fro with cruise liners calling by ... bringing new explorers. Tyneside folk are hardy, but friendly people who put up with much yet get on with the task. Community is strong here.

To me the river is an inspiration, an ever present fountain in my life with so much interest. Tyneside has a wealth of natural life and people, Geordies and all, to keep things moving on.

Through time I follow the flow of tide and river with its special bird life, assorted boats, endless folk and endeavour. I hope that you may enjoy looking at some of my Tyne photographs, selected from a period of many years which have seen lots of change on the river and in my own life. My main focus is on the lower reaches, very much influenced by tide, weather and season.

Daniel Turner
North Shields, 14 August 2016

The Sage and Tyne Bridge, Gateshead-Newcastle, 1 August 2016 : (Ref 0678) EOS 7D Mk II; EFS 17-85 mm lens; focal length 28 mm; f/20; 1/320 sec; ISO-800

'OLD SHIELDS' (1933)
WATERCOLOUR

This painting by local artist Victor Noble Rainbird (1887 - 1936) shows his ease with colour, line, shape and texture ... to capture this scene at North Shields fish quay on the River Tyne. There are reflections on the quayside, likely wet from a passing shower, while to the right lies the Gut where two or three fishing boats are berthed. A pair of foreground working fisherwomen, the one on the left perhaps with a wicker creel on her back, look out at the viewer; behind are the wooden fish sheds and tall New Low Light (operational from 1810).

Rainbird was born in North Shields and a talented artist from an early age, gaining various medals and awards as his career commenced. He served during World War One with the Northumberland Fusiliers, an experience which affected him greatly. An exhibition of some of his work was held at the Old Low Light heritage centre from July to September 2015. This was organised by the 'Friends of Victor Noble Rainbird' and Tynemouth Fine Art, with an important aim to raise funds for a fitting memorial at his otherwise unmarked Preston Cemetery grave in North Shields. The exhibition was a great success and thanks to the generosity of visitors a wonderful memorial was made, which was unveiled on 8 March 2016 (the 80th anniversary of Rainbird's death).

Image courtesy of David Hirst, Tynemouth Fine Art
(www.tynemouthfineart.com)

PART ONE

RIVER TYNE
1979 AND 1984 – 1993
SOME STORIES AND A BIT OF NOSTALGIA

The author's photographic equipment in this period comprised mainly:

Cameras   35 mm SLR film cameras: Praktica L, Praktica MTL 5, Pentax K 1000, Fujica ST 705 and Fujica ST 605

Lenses   (Praktica / Meyer), Domiplan, 50 mm, 1:2.8
                 SMC Pentax-M, 28 mm, 1:3.5
                 SMC Pentax-M, 50 mm, 1:2
                 Chinon, 135 mm, 1:2.8 (Auto Chinon)
                 Vivitar, 400 mm
                 Tamron SP, 28-135 mm, 1:4-4.5, BBAR MC
                 Tamron 300 mm, manual, 1:5.6
                 Tamron SP, 500 mm, 1:8 (Tele Macro BBAR MC)
                 Tamron SP, 2x teleconverter, BBAR MC

Light meters Weston Euro-Master II (manufactured by Megatron), plus others

Colour slide film (35 mm):   Kodak Elite 100, 200, 400; Kodachrome 64 & 200
Black and white negative film (35 mm):   Kodak Tri-X (ISO 400) and TMAX-400

Key: Photo Reference numbers   for example 81-31:
                                             81 refers to film number, and 31 is the exposure (or frame) number on that
                                             roll of film
                                             (exposures generally run from 1 to 38)

Exposure   for example f/8; 1/30 sec
                                             f/8 refers to lens aperture
                                             1/30 sec refers to shutter speed, in this case 1/30 second
                                             f/8 ½ – the ½ refers to a point halfway between f/8 and the next (smaller) f
                                             stop, in this case f/11

The photographs in the book are generally shown in date and frame order.

M A Fleming (SN 95), 1979

Trawler *M. A. Fleming* (SN 95) returns to port. This vessel was built (1948) in Hamburg of length 63 feet and with a gross tonnage of 49.

M. A. Fleming was brought to England from Germany in 1974 by Ralph Fleming who subsequently owned and skippered her from North Shields. Fisherman Kenneth Downie recalled that 'Polish' Henry brought the vessel from Germany with Ralph and the trip took six days. Ralph died at sea aboard his boat, in his bunk, of a heart attack. He had named the boat after his wife Martha Ann Fleming. His wife later sold her to the FMA (Fishermen's Mutual Association). After Ralph, a new skipper followed ... 'Polish' Henry (a North Shields fish quay character) and then Richard ('Dicky') Leighton followed in 1975 – his first boat as a ticketed skipper. Richard skippered her for a year or so, while the boat was owned by the FMA, Boston Deep Sea and by her next owner Barry Moss, who bought her in 1976-77. A later skipper was James Cullen (of North Shields). Richard Leighton recalled fishing her on 3-5 day trips to the Dab Hole. He also recollected that she was a riveted vessel of black iron (a type of steel) and had undergone work in Germany, prior to arrival in England, during which she was cut in half amidships and an extra ten feet was welded into the hull. Previous owner Barry Moss had a recollection that the vessel was originally built for the German Navy and later converted into a fishing vessel. Barry fished her in the winter and carried out diving and salvage work with her in the summer. After Barry Moss, her next owner was Geoffrey Hardaker. She was seen in recent years as a hulk on the south coast of England. When fishing from northern England *M A Fleming* was thought to have made little money, was a difficult boat to work ... and killed her owner Ralph Fleming. Not a good record!

The skipper of wooden trawler *Nordland* had stopped her in the dark near the Tyne south pier end to adjust his variable pitch propeller, with which he was having trouble, when an arriving Whitby boat, *Ard Aidam*, collided with her and she started taking on water. A Tyne pilot boat towed *Nordland* close to the south pier, where she sank. This incident happened in the late 1970s to early 1980s. Barry Moss got the job, from the Port of Tyne Authority, of retrieving the sunken *Nordland* for salvage ... which he did with the use of *M. A. Fleming* under skipper James Cullen. The remains of the boat were brought to the beach at South Shields, broken up and burnt, with permission ... the wind was offshore (westerly). Barry gave the *Nordland* nameplate to the New Dolphin pub at North Shields fish quay and it has subsequently gone to a new owner along with the boat's wheel.

Tyne river mouth, June 1979 : (Photo Ref 41-33) Kodachrome slide film; f/5.6; 1/250 sec

NORDLAND, RESTING ON SOUTH SHIELDS BEACH

When the *Nordland* (GY 237) sank, the top of her mast showed above the water at first. The next day a buoy was placed beside her to warn of the new hazard. Then the *M A Fleming*, under skipper James (Jimmy) Cullen, dragged her onto the beach at South Shields on a high tide, inside of the South pier. It took a month or so for Barry Moss and his team to break her up and burn the wooden boat. The local council gave permission for the boat to be burnt as long as a westerly wind was blowing offshore. The engine was driven away by Billy Blevings, on a heavy goods vehicle, and scrapped. Billy worked with Barry for many years.

Photograph courtesy of Barry Moss; photographer unknown.

Basking shark

The North Shields News Guardian, dated Thursday 26 July 1984, states:

Shark caught

'A 22-foot long basking shark was landed at North Shields Fish Quay by coble *Coquet Star* this week. The shark was sold in large portions to several merchants by skipper Mr Derek Heselton of Romilly Street, South Shields.'

The basking shark (*Cetorhinus maximus*) is a filter feeder on plankton; its huge liver can account for a quarter of its weight. It is the second largest living fish (the largest is the whale shark, *Rhincodon typus*, a tropical species which also feeds on plankton). The brick building beyond the shark housed the fish quay public conveniences which were demolished in March 2007. The shark is resting on a blue bogey; these were intended for boats using agent Caley Fisheries (red ones were for Irvin's boats).

Basking shark on Union Quay, North Shields fish quay, 23 July 1984 : (Photo Ref 81-31); f/5.6; 1/250 sec

KEN GIBSON AND AIRCRAFT PROPELLER

Ken Gibson stands beside an aircraft propeller brought back from a North Sea fishing trip by one of the North Shields boats. A retired fish quay worker thought the boat was *Coastal Pioneer* (H 92) though the author found a note with his photograph which stated, 'Dragged up by *Polar Wind* last week'. Terry Reed (see page 88) remembers this gentleman as 'Ken the waterman' who worked for the Port of Tyne Authority (PTA). Ken would wheel a heavy rolled hose around the main quay and the western quay to attach and supply water to the fishing boats, in turn.

At the western quay there was a water point beside the fuel berth, but there were several on the main quay. Terry told the author that when he started working on the fish quay for Purdy's, in 1972, he remembered that Ken was already working on the quay at that time and continued to work there for many more years. Terry said Ken was 'old school' and 'a gentleman' and likely assisted part-time as a quaymaster too. There is another photograph of Ken Gibson, by the author, on page 22.

North Shields fish quay, 2 December 1984 : (Photo Ref 87-26); f/5.6; 1/30 sec

HALIBUT

The author was told, at the time he took the photograph, that this was a mock halibut otherwise known as Greenland halibut, presumably landed by a boat at North Shields. It is, however, considered to be a specimen of the (Atlantic) halibut *Hippoglossus hippoglossus*, which can live up to 40-50 years and grow to a maximum length of 3-4 metres. Currently endangered and with no fishing quota, any landed are sadly trawler by-catch. Halibut is described as 'a roaming, bottom-living fish in depths of 50-2,000 metres ...' and with a very well-flavoured flesh (Muus & Dahlstrøm, 1974). This halibut was hanging outside Hadaway's fish shop (North Shields) which was owned and run by North Shields playwright Tom Hadaway (1923-2005). Tom was born Hunter, but his surname changed to Hadaway after adoption; his stepfather, Tom Hadaway senior, ran Hadaway's shop on Rudyerd Street as early as the 1920s. Tom (junior, the playwright) was a fish merchant who first put pen to paper aged 40, using his experiences in the fish trade. He enjoyed great success writing plays for theatre and television. The fish shop was later owned by Chris Thompson ... when one of the suppliers was Paul Spivey (of Spivey's Shellfish).

Hadaway's fish shop, Rudyerd, Street, North Shields, 3 April 1985 : (Photo Ref 93-26) Kodak Elite 200; f/2.8 ½; 1/250 sec

Lloyds jetty and installing new pipe (sewer outlet)

Wooden Lloyds jetty, no longer used to record Tyne shipping movements, but left to the birds. A watch house was opened in 1902 at the end of the jetty by Lloyds of London. The watch house was manned until 1969 and here it was recorded where ships were bound, when arriving on and departing from the Tyne, for legal requirements, before later methods were adopted. A new section of pipe is shown being fitted from the sewer system overflow so the water would run out to the end of the jetty and into the Tyne, instead of simply pouring onto the shore. For many years sewage ran onto the beach here – attracting feeding gulls and rats. The work shown was undertaken during the period of the Tyne interceptor sewer project when raw sewage outfalls into the Tyne were diverted to the treatment works at East Howdon. Following the commissioning of the Tyneside Sewage Treatment scheme in 1970 and completion of the work in 1993, Tyne salmon rod catches were seen to rise from zero (or very low figures) in 1960 to 246 in 1982, 1898 in 1999 and increasing to annual catches of 3,000 – 4,000 fish in the period 2004 – 2009.

North Shields fish quay, 20 April 1985 : (Photo Ref 95-33) Kodak Elite 400; f/8; 1/250 sec

ALBERT EDWARD DOCK

The photograph shows Albert Edward Dock, North Shields on 14 April 1985. This is now home to the Royal Quays Marina (opened in late 1998) and is surrounded by the Royal Quays housing development. The brick building to the left (with four windows) was the power house with machinery to power the hydraulics and operate the dock gates to allow craft in and out (Larry Irvine worked there). The narrow sandstone tower (left of centre) was a hydraulic accumulator built in 1882 to hold a head of water to provide pressure in the operation of the dock (and lock) gates. It still stands with clock faces and is a Grade II Listed Building. Sir W G Armstrong (1810 – 1900) first developed this type of hydraulic machinery in Newcastle during the late 1840s and this is the only surviving example on the Tyne. It is said that 'The hydraulic accumulator was one of Armstrong's greatest inventions, if not the most spectacular' (McKenzie 1983). The cranes in the picture are long gone. Behind where the author stood to take the photograph was a large area of derelict land (previously Tyne Commissioners Standage Ground) which had supported waggon and railways allowing coal, brought from southeast Northumberland mines, to be shipped away. Coal wagons offloaded their cargo into ships from the large wooden staithes, whose remnants run into the dock from lower left corner of the photograph. These Dene Staithes are no more – there was an upper level raising them to the height of the surrounding land for the waggons. The dock offices, to right of picture with windows on three levels, and quayside sheds have gone. North Sea ferry tickets were sold from one of these offices while one was later an education centre. The taller of these two office buildings housed the Port of Tyne Authority at one time. A modern boat yard now stands in the main left foreground of the photograph. The long dark shed (central distance) was the Bergen Quay shed near which was the Oslo berth. The author used to visit the derelict waggon way land here during and following the 1970s by bicycle, and later by motorcycle, to view its flora and fauna.

Larry Irvine operated the dock gates for about fifteen years, from 1972, following time working on the Shields ferry. The author got to know Larry during his time at Albert Edward Dock. Larry told the story of a seagull (herring gull) which had injured a wing a little before he started work at the dock (1972). Other gulls were attacking the injured one and Bob Penaluna (a local liberal councillor) caught the bird and put splints on it to help with the healing process. The gull was then kept in a small hut on the middle pier, between the lock gates, so it may recover, and they named it Sammy. It became a bit like a pet and Larry would feed it; the wing healed and it was able to fly again and Larry said, "It became the dominant gull of the area," where it remained for another ten years or so. In the summer it would depart, perhaps to South Shields to nest and it would bring its young back to the dock, "sometimes it had two. It loved cheese," Larry mentioned, "and it would come when you called it. Sometimes its wing hung down." One day it was found dead – young lads with air rifles had shot it. Larry had brought food for it that day and was told, "Sammy's in the skip, dead." The staff were upset and very annoyed. A local bird recorder came to weigh Sammy and said it was one and a half times heavier than a normal gull; Larry thought, "Perhaps that was because we fed it."

Portrait photo: Larry Irvine, North Shields, 15 July 2016 : (Photo Ref 6742) EOS 30D; EFS 17-85 mm lens; focal length 61 mm; f/9; 1/50 sec; ISO-1000

Albert Edward Dock, North Shields, 14 April 1985 : (Photo Ref 95-30) Kodak Elite 400; f/8 ½; 1/125 sec
There is a wonderful colour photo (by Dennis Maccoy) taken from almost the same viewpoint on 5 July 1968; see … http://www.tynebuiltships.co.uk/S-Ships/southshields1911.html

FISHERMAN WITH CALEY'S BOXES FULL OF FISH

One of the crew from *Mayflower IV* (LH 257; a visiting boat) helps to land her catch which was stored in Caley Fisheries wooden boxes. This vessel was built in 1974 at Arbroath of length 57 feet.

North Shields fish quay, 5 July 1985 : (Photo Ref 105-16) Kodak Elite 200; f/8; 1/60 sec

LOADING *SHARONA* (LH 263) WITH EMPTY BOXES

A crew member from *Sharona* (LH 263) helps load empty fish boxes aboard for the next trip. *Sharona* was built in 1980 at Campbeltown of length 70 feet and with a gross tonnage of 50. *Sharona* was one of four boats owned by the Moodie family from the Leith area. The four boats were *Sharona*, *Shemarah*, *Sharon Rose* and *Rose of Sharon*; they were skippered by four sons and regularly worked from Shields during the eighties. All four boats were dealt with through the Caley Fisheries office for many years until they set up their own office somewhere in Granton.

Caley Fisheries is a ships' agent which provides auctioneering services, runs a chandlery, etc., as well as servicing the financial and administration needs of the boat owners and fishermen. Richard Irvin and Sons as well as Caley Fisheries would have shares in some of the boats and/or help owners/skippers with the financing of boats (Nautilus Consultants 1990).

North Shields fish quay, 9 September 1985 : (Photo Ref 119-03) Kodak Elite 400; f/8 ½; 1/125 sec

HERRING SELLERS' MARKET BEFORE DEMOLITION (1)

Herring were landed at the Western Quay, North Shields, and part of the catch (perhaps a sample comprising half a basket) from each boat was brought in small metal and plastic boxes featuring the name Croan (Croan Seafoods Ltd) to the herring market. Here bids were made for the boat's full catches ... many buyers could purchase from each boat. Auctioneers sold the herring on behalf of the fishing boats which would then be paid through an agent such as Purdy, Caley or Irvin. Fish merchant John Ellis recalled that ... in the morning all the kipper house owners, of which there were about seventeen in the 1950s, would come to the market and sit on the benches where an Irvin's man auctioned the fish. The herring were tipped, in turn, from the baskets onto a scale so the buyers could check size, weight and quality. Bill Bridge (see page 57) remembered that a bell was rung, to attract the buyers, before the herring market sales began in the morning.

The herring sellers' market building was likely built in the 1920s and it served a dual purpose. As well as being used to sell herring, at night time it had a secondary role. Around ten o'clock in the evening the 'buskers' would come ... buskers were fish quay workers who helped land the boats' catches – there were thousands of boxes of fish landed during the 1950s and 1960s requiring many buskers. The buskers would sit on the herring market benches and the foremen from Irvin's, Purdy, Hastie, etc. would come to pick a squad of men to work overnight. They would be paid in the morning, perhaps one guinea plus a fry up of half a dozen large haddock and a similar number of herring. Several of the old kipper (or smoke) houses still exist on the fish quay, but not necessarily now used in the smoking of fish; John Ellis could recollect about ten such houses up Tanners Bank.

Herring Sellers' Market, North Shields fish quay, 14 September 1985 : (Photo Ref 119-09) Kodak Elite 400; f/4; 1/30 sec

Herring Sellers' Market before demolition (2)
North Shields fish quay, 14 September 1985 : (Photo Ref 119-13) Kodak Elite 400; f/8 ½; 1/60 sec

KEN GIBSON PORTRAIT, WATERMAN

This is waterman Ken Gibson (see page 13). The author would be interested to hear from anyone able to provide more information on Ken.

The background scene is of the fish market shed; since this photograph was taken the shed and market have been substantially altered. There was originally an upper floor to the market area with offices and stores, for example in which to keep fish boxes. It is thought the upper floor was demolished in the period 1968-72 and replaced by the market shed as seen in this photograph. According to Dodds (2013), '... a covered fish market, erected by Tynemouth Corporation, opened on the fish quay in 1897 ...'

North Shields fish quay, 28 September 1985: (Photo Ref 116-16); 135 mm lens; f/8; 1/125 sec

NORTH SHIELDS BOX POOL (NSBP) BOXES

North Shields Box Pool wooden fish boxes, made on the quay – they are all plastic nowadays. Richard Irvin and Sons Limited managed the North Shields Box Pool.

North Shields fish quay, 15 September 1985: (Photo Ref 119-22) Kodak Elite 400; f/8 ½; 1/125 sec

TREVOR FRYER AND INSHORE LIFEBOAT

Tynemouth lifeboat volunteer Trevor Fryer checking the inshore lifeboat (ILB: D-280) beside the RNLI crew's storage (or 'watch') house (now demolished) near Lloyds jetty. The inshore lifeboat was housed in a brick building beside Fish Quay Sands, ready for launch at short notice. The shadowy entrance to this brick storage building (it looked like a car garage) is visible behind the lifeboat to the right of picture. This was Mark II (or version 2) of the ILB house and its entrance faced upriver. In Mark I the entrance had faced the river, but the building was demolished and washed away in a storm; the ILB was washed away with it and ended up near the current lifeboat station entrance gate. D class inshore boat D-280 served with Tynemouth lifeboat station from 1982 – 1989.

North Shields fish quay, 13 October 1985 : (Photo Ref 118-16) Kodak Elite 100; f/8; 1/125 sec

SIR TRISTRAM SHIP'S LIFEBOAT

The photograph shows a ship's lifeboat from RFA *Sir Tristram* (L3505) which served in the Falklands War and was badly damaged on 8 June 1982 at Fitzroy when strafed and bombed by A-4 Skyhawks from the Argentine Air Force. RFA *Sir Tristram* was a Sir Lancelot Class Landing Ship Logistics vessel, built on the Tyne at Hawthron Leslie and launched in December 1966. Following the Falklands War she was extensively rebuilt and re-entered active service concluding in 2005, but subsequently used in a static training role with Maritime Special Forces. This ship's lifeboat, seen here under private ownership, was converted into a local pleasure craft. Of the three cobles on the river behind, the blue one in the middle is *Freya* (SN 121, built in Seaton Sluice), then owned by Brian Telford of North Shields. Brian owned her as a pleasure craft for about five years.

Fish Quay Sands, North Shields fish quay, 24 May 1986 : (Photo Ref 129-10) Kodak Elite 200; 50 mm; f/11; 1/125 sec

MINESWEEPER *ORWELL* AND RIG

HMS *Orwell* (named after the River Orwell in Suffolk) was launched in 1985; a River-class minesweeper. She was sold to Guyana in 2001 and renamed *Essequibo* (which is the name of a Guyanese river). The jack-up rig (*Ocean* *Benarmin*; now named *Ensco 72*) in the background was at McNulty Yard, South Shields. On the right of the picture is the long yellow leg from one of the mobile cranes that worked on the quay here.

Tyne Commission Quay (now Northumbrian Quay), North Shields, 25 May 1986 : (Photo Ref 129-15) Kodak Elite 200; f/8 ½; 1/250 sec

TUG – *SEASIDER*

Tug *Seasider* was built of steel construction by Richard Dunston (Hessle) Ltd (on the River Humber) and launched in December 1984, working on the river Tyne from 1985 to c.1995. On the Tyne she was employed by Tyne Tugs Ltd and later by Tyne & Wear Tugs Ltd. She went to Greece in 1999 and was still noted as in service in 2014.

Passing Tyne Commission Quay (now Northumbrian Quay), North Shields, 25 May 1986 : (Photo Ref 129-28) Kodak Elite 200; 135 mm

TUG – *ANGLIANMAN*

Tugboat *Anglianman* is shown here under the ownership of Klyne-Winney Tugs (Lowestoft) which was soon to cease trading and become Klyne Tugs (Lowestoft) Ltd until this company was sold to J P Knight in 2007. *Anglianman* was built on the river Humber as *Motorman* (launched in 1965); she had two sister tugs called *Anglian* (launched in 1964 as *Tugman*) and *Trawlerman* (launched in 1962).

All three were built and launched by Humber St. Andrews Engineering Company Ltd, Hull, for United Towing Ltd of Hull. *Anglianman* was with Klyne-Winney Tugs from 1984 to 1988 then sold to a Hartlepool company and renamed *Clevelandman* with further owners to follow; she was still in service in 2010, of length 83 feet nine inches and beam 24 feet and one inch.

Klyne Tugs converted the three sister boats from river tugs to coastal towing tugs by fitting winches and converting two cabins on the main deck, below the bridge, to a mess room for the comfort of the crew. They were twin screw vessels each with two, six-cylinder Lister Blackstone main engines. They were used for coastal towage of barges and worked with dredging companies on various UK projects. *Anglianman* was also involved on a sea defence project near Clacton (Essex) towing barges loaded with rock from an offshore delivery barge to the coast.

In the early 1980s Roger Klyne, of Lowestoft, moved from the fishery and fish trade to towage – and began with Mr Winney and two small tugs as Klyne & Winney Tugs. By 1988 Mr Winney had dropped out of the picture and the tugs were taken over by Klyne Tugs (Lowestoft) Ltd. By 2001 the company had grown into Britain's largest independent tug operator (van der Meljden 2002).

The fishing boat in the background is *Helga Risager* (WA 45) – she was built in Buckie in 1956 of 63 feet in length (see page 30 for more detail).

North Shields fish quay, 26 May 1986 : (Photo Ref 130-09) Kodak Elite 100; f/11; 1/125 sec

Tug – *Northsider*

Retired Tyne tugboat man John Sturmey recalled some facts for the author, recounted here. Tug *Northsider* was built in the late 1960s and served on the Tyne into the 1990s before being sold with her sister tug, *Ironsider*, to Greece where she is still thought to be working. *Northsider* worked for 'Lawson-Batey Tugs Ltd' … one of three companies operating tugs under the colours of Tyne Tugs Limited. The other two companies were 'France, Fenwick Tyne & Wear Co Ltd' and 'Ridley Tugs Ltd'. John was a Tyne tugboat man from 1959 to 1970, and started by working aboard steam tug *Eastsider* operating with Lawson-Batey Tugs.

Entering the river, 21 June 1986 : (Photo Ref 144-24) Tamron 300 mm lens; Kodak Tri-X; f/11 ½; 1/500 sec

HELGA RISAGER COMING IN TO HARBOUR

The fishing boat to right of picture is *Helga Risager* (WA 45; registered in Whitehaven) – built in Buckie in 1956 of 63 feet (see page 28-29). At North Shields *Helga Risager* had several owners, one was Alan Laurie (also known as 'Bubbles'); at first Eric Robinson was skipper, then Bob Brown became skipper from 1989 to 1998. She was Bob's last boat as a skipper and was later decommissioned; since then Bob has worked on supply vessels offshore. Several quite successful big North Shields boats were decommissioned around the same time as *Helga Risager* because fishing restrictions and quota changes made their continuance in fishing inviable. When Bob was skipper, in the summer they may go for five- to six-day trips, while in the winter time it was one-day trips for prawns from 5 a.m. to 5 p.m. When berthed at the fish quay she was never locked and fishermen would often

sleep aboard if they had nowhere else to go. Due to this – she became known as the 'Hotel *Risager*'. Local fisherman Keith Harvey (pages 86-87) was one of her crew working on one- to three-day sea trips.

Skipper Bob Brown mentioned that Alan Laurie was, "known to be [careful] with money and did a lot of good turns for other fishermen." For example he would help with engines on other boats. He was also reported to have had a shellfish / crab processing factory near the Wolsington House public house, Appleby Street (N Shields), was a "canny man" and aged about sixty when he died.

In addition this photograph shows Lloyds jetty end, with its resting winter cormorants, and visiting Scottish fishing boat *Auriga III* (LH 449).

Running for the fish quay, 28 December 1989 : (Photo Ref 187-13) Vivitar 400 mm lens; Kodak TMAX-400; f/11; 1/250 sec

RAFT RACE

One of the rafts (*Hellsinky Mk II*), with a ladies crew arriving beside Fish Quay Sands during the Bank Holiday Monday raft race from New Quay, North Shields. The race was organised by Tyne and Wear Playing Fields Association and due to start at 11 a.m. – billed to include eleven rafts launched from the Jim Marine slipway beside the ferry landing. During the previous three years the race had raised over £2,000 for projects including those benefitting handicapped children. On the side of the raft is the text 'Stockdale D C'. This must be the Stockdale Day Centre of Osborne Gardens, North Shields; opened on 30 April 1969 and closed in autumn 1993 due to cuts imposed to meet government spending restrictions. The Stockdale Centre, run by North Tyneside Council, was a social and handicraft centre for the physically disabled, named after architect William Stockdale (of Howard Street, North Shields) who did much for charity and produced a sketch plan of the centre.

North Shields fish quay, 26 May 1986 : (Photo Ref 130-06) Kodak Elite 100; 300 mm Tamron lens; f/11 ½; 1/125 sec

Frem (GY 325) LIFEBELT AND FLARE

Frem (GY 325) fished from North Shields regularly at this time. She was built in 1939 at Frederikshavn (Denmark) of length 57 feet with a gross tonnage of 25; owned locally by Nat Herd (senior) and handled through the agents Richard Irvin and Sons Limited.

The vessel was built for Nat Herd (senior) who sailed her over from Denmark before the Germans occupied the country (from April 1940) during World War Two. The *Frem* had a gun mounted on her bow, when first built, and when Nat fished her from northern Scottish waters she was attacked occasionally by German fighters. Nat Herd (senior) fished her from Grimsby, North Shields and Scotland, and would also run her on fishing trips up to Iceland. She was sold to Frank Malloy, who had her for about five years, before he sold her to Nat Herd (junior) and his stepson Paul Wenn. Nat and Paul fished her for about five years from North Shields in the 1980s … anchor seine netting and trawling, on one week fishing trips. Paul told the author, "It was very hard work. We used ropes in the day and trawled at night." Nat Herd (junior) was skipper during this time when the crew of four mainly fished for flatfish … plaice and lemon sole.

See page 49 for more information on *Frem*.

North Shields fish quay, 26 May 1986, lifebelt and flare : (Photo Ref 130-16) Kodak Elite 100; 135 mm lens; f/11 ½; 1/125 sec

FREM – REGISTRATION NUMBER (GY 325)

Frem (GY 325) was registered at Grimsby port (GY) with fishing number 325, but regularly fishing from North Shields.

North Shields fish quay, 26 May 1986, registration number : (Photo Ref 130-12) Kodak Elite 100; f/5.6 ½; 1/125 sec

BOGEY

Wooden bogey, pulled by hand, for carrying boxes of fish and loose fish (by using a wooden surround), etc. Fish merchant John Ellis recalled that a full bogey may weigh a ton – the fish quay workers were very fit having to haul these around all day – they must have had muscles on their muscles! Once a common sight on the fish quay, these bogeys have now all gone ... the forklifts do it nowadays, lifting boxes on wooden pallets. This is a red bogey and therefore intended for boats using agent Richard Irvin and Sons Ltd.

North Shields fish quay, 31 May 1986 : (Photo Ref 130-29) Kodak Elite 100; f/5.6; 1/30 sec

GOLDEN RAY

This vessel seems to be a restored fishing boat, called *Golden Ray*, from Hartlepool; she was possibly visiting the Tyne for the Tall Ships event later in the month. When based at Hartlepool (ca. 1970s) the fishing boat was owned by Frank Bergan. *Golden Ray* is seen here, from North Shields fish quay, passing the old pilot boat station (now known as No 4 Groyne) at South Shields where a river pilot boat (thought to be *Lady Hayward*) can be seen waiting. The yellow structure, towards left of picture, is the tower of the South Shields Volunteer Life Brigade watch house, built in 1867. The building with the white stripe, directly behind the wheelhouse of *Golden Ray*, is the old Radar Training School. At the time of the picture the pilot boats were run by the Tyne Pilotage Authority; responsibility for pilotage did not transfer to the Port of Tyne until 1988.

Passing North Shields fish quay, 6 July 1986 : (Photo Ref 131-08) Kodak Elite 400; 135 mm; f/11; 1/250 sec

AVONDALE, SHOWING VELVA LIQUIDS

This boat was called *Avondale* and came from Scotland; a local lad, Alan Lopez, owned her ... she was a Caley Fisheries vessel. Alan sold her to Joe Gilmour (of Sunderland) who owned her when she sank 30 miles off North Shields. One of her local 'deckies' was Ephraim Fenwick Mundy (senior). Ephraim is a Hebrew name, pronounced EE-frim, and means *double fruitfulness*. Ephraim (senior) and his son Ephraim Fenwick Mundy (junior, known as Fen) fished, off and on, aboard *Border Maid II* (AH 117) while she was based at North Shields, for a period of 17 years from 1970, under skipper and part-owner George Crawford. Ephraim (senior) was also relief skipper of the *Border Maid II* when George Crawford was poorly. *Border Maid II* was built by Gerards of Arbroath in 1970, she was 54 feet with a 230 hp Gardner engine and a wooden hull. When Ephraim (senior and junior) fished with her – in the summer they seine-netted and in the winter they bobbin trawled i.e. worked hard ground. The

Border Maid II replaced an earlier *Border Maid*, on which Fen (junior) had one fishing trip.

The large tanks in the background, on the south side of the river at South Shields opposite the fish quay, were part of the Velva Liquids site. In one of the tanks (tank number 2), for the storage of petrol, a preserved body (torso and head) was found when the tank was being cleaned out in 1979, and determined to be that of sixteen or seventeen year old Eileen McDougall who had gone missing in 1970 – she had died from head injuries. Ernest Adolphus Clarke, from Hull, a previous Velva employee was charged with her murder and served 14 years; he was released at the age of 63 and in frail health. There was some concern that Ernest Clarke may have been innocent and had been convicted unfairly; he had pleaded not guilty, though an appeal hearing also found him guilty.

Departing the river, passing North Shields fish quay, 15 July 1986 : (Photo Ref 131-14) Kodak Elite 400; 135 mm; f/22; 1/250 sec

LAURA EVE, LUC AND NORTHUMBRIAN WATER

Laura Eve (SN 54; a Caley Fisheries boat) was built in 1986 at Dunston on Tyne of length 38 feet and with a gross tonnage of 28; so, very new in this photograph. She was owned by brothers John and Robert Kelly and skippered by Denis Cave; there were sister ships *Rochelle* and *Phaeton I* ... 12 metre steel boats. John Kelly went on to become an engineer. To left of picture, part of *Luc* (SN 36) shows while passing upriver is ship *Northumbrian Water*.

Northumbrian Water was built by Ailsa Shipbuilding Company on the River Clyde in 1977, a sludge carrier of length 237.8 feet and deadweight 1654 tons. She spent her life owned by Northumbrian Water Authority (Newcastle), serving on the Tyne and dumping sewage sludge, from the treatment works at East Howdon, out at sea. She was towed from Sunderland to Lowestoft for scrapping in early 2016.

North Shields fish quay, 18 July 1986 : (Photo Ref 130-36) Kodak Elite 100; f/11; 1/125 sec

LOYAL VOLUNTEER (A 160)

Loyal Volunteer (A 160) was built in the late 1970s as a training vessel for the Royal Naval Auxiliary Service (RNXS) as a Loyal Class vessel. At one time she was based at Upnor (Kent), across the River Medway from Chatham Dockyard and also recorded as based at Rosyth. She was also reported to have sailed out of Sunderland, Newcastle and Blyth and noted to have sailed from Sunderland to Newcastle to view the tall ships when they were in northeast England in 1986. *Loyal Volunteer* was photographed from North Shields fish quay as she passed upriver with South Shields in the background.

Sailing upriver past South Shields, opposite North Shields fish quay, 28 February 1987 :
(Photo Ref 147-22) Kodak Elite 200; f/8 ½; 1/250 sec

New High and Low lights with scaffolding

The photograph shows the New High Light and its partner the New Low Light (both built ca. 1806 – 1810) with scaffolding for renovations and a fresh coat of white paint. The guiding lights in these two lighthouses were aligned by vessels entering the river, to avoid hitting the ever-present rocks and sand banks. The low building with four windows, this side of the New Low Light, was once a lifeboat house, then a telegraph office and later a café, now gone. Retired fisherman Keith Harvey (pages 86-87) recalled that a lady called Ella Small ran the café and she would cook fish for you if you took some in. "You had to take four pieces," Keith recalled, "and you would get two back, cooked, with chips. She kept the rest!" Ella was known to be a grafter and her husband was called Billy Germaine ... who was a quaymaster. Working with Ella in the café were two other women ... Jean and Joan. Jean would warm her slippers in the café oven while a fish quay cat ... "sat on top of the grill on top of the oven, to keep warm," Keith reminisced. He also told the author that in the early morning, after the fish market sales, the fish buyers sat in the café drinking tea and playing dominoes (the main players were: Ronnie Longstaff, John MacDonald, Victor [Armstrong?] and someone from Wright & Eddie). Behind the New Low Light (in the picture) is corrugated grey fencing behind which stood the quaymaster offices in a 'Portacabin'.

North Shields fish quay, 9 May 1987 :
(Photo Ref 150-15) Practika MTL-5; 50 mm lens;
Kodak Elite 400; f/11; 1/250 sec

THE GUT, FIRST FISH QUAY FESTIVAL

The Gut with local fishing boats dressed for the first Fish Quay Festival. On the left are: *Luc* (SN 36; closest to quayside) and *P'Tit Moine* (J 43; built in France, 1964). On the right are: *Christine Nielsen* (GY 298; built in Denmark, 1975), *Snowflake* (SN 1; built in Gardenstown, 1948) and *Silver Echo* (LH 453; built in Eyemouth, 1967). The colourful fish on the bankside were an early prototype for the full sculpture and mosaics (Naters Bank Fishscape), whose installation was well underway in September 1987 by FreeForm Arts.

North Shields fish quay, 23 May 1987 : (Photo Ref 151-28) Pentax K 1000; Kodak Elite 200

GALLANT VENTURE (SN 4), FISH QUAY FESTIVAL

Local Caley Fisheries fishing boat *Gallant Venture* (SN 4; owned by John Moyle from Sunderland), dressed for the fish quay festival, passing the fish quay. An estimated 50,000 visitors came to attend the two day event (Sat-Sun, 23-24 May), and discussions followed about making it annual. On the Saturday morning came a parade of the fishing fleet while Sunday brought the Blessing of the Fleet service – with many other activities during the weekend and fireworks, mid-river, on Saturday evening. The fleet parade brought the dressed fishing boats upriver to Newcastle and back to the fish quay. Author Peter Mortimer, from Cullercoats, published his book 'The last of the hunters' to coincide with the fishing festival.

North Shields fish quay, 23 May 1987 : (Photo Ref 151-14) Pentax K 1000; Kodak Elite 200

Hedwin, Tyne dredger

Hedwin was a grab hopper dredger of length 157 feet, launched in March 1969 and owned by the Port of Tyne Authority. She was built by the Leith Shipyards of Robb Caledonian Shipbuilders Ltd. *Hedwin* was used to dredge the Tyne and keep it navigable for river traffic; she worked here for 42 years and was then sold to work in West Africa under the name of *KMC Pelican*.

North Shields fish quay, 28 June 1987 : (Photo Ref 152-30) Pentax K 1000; Kodak Elite 200; f/8 ½; 1/125 sec

HEDWIN, HOPPER FULL OF MUD

The *Hedwin*, here shown with a hopper full of mud ... after dredging and using her grab in the river Tyne. The material she dredged from the river was generally unloaded a few miles out to sea, but some of the more unusual items may be separated out. These included such things as: an articulated lorry trailer, safes, a sports car, an ingot and a bronze cannon (Chaplin & Tiernan 2010).

North Shields fish quay, 28 June 1987 : (Photo Ref 152-34) Kodak Elite 200; f/8 ½; 1/60 sec

FISH QUAY MARKET, SALES ABOUT TO START

Richard Irvin auctioneer and manager, Bill Ponton, in white coat, waits to sell well-packed haddock stored with ice in wooden fish boxes of the North Shields Box Pool. Bill is the oldest brother of Martin Ponton (of William Wight Ltd., Union Quay, North Shields). The gentleman (with red top) in centre is Joe Parks, who went on to work for Vic Armstrong (AA Fisheries) from the late 1980s. Joe Parks worked for Ross Fish during the 1980s and then with Maconochie Seafoods (a Hull based company run by Nev Hewison), AA Fisheries and then other fish quay merchants. On the right, with dark top and back to us is David ('Davy') Chatterton and next to him in grey top is Norman Brant, both men are wearing pale blue jeans. Norman and David worked for Maconochie Seafoods (where the Aroma coffee house stands now on Union Quay). Fish merchant John Ellis recalled that David Chatterton and Alan Hall were partners in a fish quay business at one time.

North Shields fish quay, 24 September 1987 : (Photo Ref 157-10) Kodak Elite 400

KIM DAVID (SN 166)

Kim David (SN 166), pictured here just off the fish quay with South Shields in the background; built in 1947 (Denmark) of length 42 feet. New local owners Edward Higgins and Cliff Brand bought her from Esbjerg (Denmark); she was brought to North Shields and re-registered. Of typical Danish wooded build with a 150 hp Callesen marine diesel engine and rigged as a gill-netter. Under Cliff and Edward's ownership the boat was skippered by Trevor Senior who then bought her with the help of agent Richard Irvin and Sons Ltd. She had continued as a gill-netter from North Shields, but when sold to Trevor she was converted to inshore trawling for prawns and persisted in this for a few years. Hilla Kay had been a crew member from North Shields for two months; another deckie (deckhand) had the nickname 'Tiger'. There are two different stories about her final demise: one recounts of being de-commissioned, the other (by a previous owner) that she sank at sea. Skipper Trevor Senior passed his knowledge to son Darren, who now owns *Emily Rose* (SN 85) and previously *Charisma* (BH 27) and *Still Waters* (SN 85).

North Shields fish quay, 25 September 1987 :
(Photo Ref 157-24) Kodak Elite 400; f/16;
1/250 sec

SIRIUS, GREENPEACE SHIP ON THE TYNE

The photograph shows Greenpeace ship *Sirius* (registered in Amsterdam) passing upriver, with South Shields behind, on 25 September 1987. In August 1987, Greenpeace launched an eight-week action campaign against ocean incineration, the burning of hazardous waste, particularly highly toxic polychlorinated biphenyls (PCBs), in furnaces aboard ships at sea. During this campaign their activists boarded incinerator ship *Vesta* and attempted to board another called *Vulcanus II*, both in the North Sea, and prevented them from burning their cargo. It was during this activity when *Sirius* came into the Tyne. MV *Sirius* was named after the star of the same name, built in 1950 in the Netherlands as a pilot vessel and originally owned by the Royal Dutch Navy. She was sold to Greenpeace in 1981, retiring in 1998; then served in an educational capacity while docked at Amsterdam.

Passing North Shields fish quay, 25 September 1987 : (Photo Ref 157-30) Kodak Elite 400; f/16; 1/250 sec

Forklift truck and driver

Driver with forklift truck, carrying plastic fish boxes along Bell St, near Quayside Court – the boxes filled with ice from the ice plant of the Western Quay. There were few forklifts on the fish quay at this time and Caley Fisheries had one or two. However this is not a Caley's forklift as it has a registration plate, but Caley's forklifts were not registered, so had no plate. The registration looks like A 661 BJR; the prefix 'A' registration was introduced in 1983. The manufacturer name printed on this forklift is Datsun ... a Japanese company with its roots in the early twentieth century. After selling 20 million cars in 190 countries around the world, the Datsun brand was phased out in 1981 and the Nissan name used as the company expanded globally. In March 2012 Nissan announced the return of the Datsun brand. At the time of going to print the name of the forklift driver and the company he worked for are unknown. If you can help with further information please contact the author.

North Shields fish quay, 25 September 1987 : (Photo Ref 157-35) Kodak Elite 400; f/22; 1/250 sec

Fuel point, Western Quay

Fishing vessels called for fuel at the Western Quay, North Shields, at the location shown here. The North Tyneside Council report (1988) mentions … 'Fuel bunker (Esso), operated by Richard Irvin and Sons at west end of general trade berth with draught of 5.01 m supplying Esso Marine Diesel, Marine Gas Oil and Marine Lubricants.' Fuel is currently supplied there by Caley Fisheries. Caley's bought the fuel depot from Richard Irvin and Sons in the early nineties and ran it until Caley's sold out to Northern Oils several years ago. Northern Oils retained the Caley Oils name, however they went into administration in 2015 and now, having gone full circle, the fuel depot is back in Caley's hands. At the depot marine gas oil is dispensed mainly to fishing boats as well as work boats, pleasure craft and forklift trucks. Gas oil (red diesel) and unleaded petrol are also supplied to boats by Quay Marinas Ltd at the Royal Quays fuel pontoon.

North Shields fish quay, 25 September 1987 : (Photo Ref 157-38) Kodak Elite 400; f/22; 1/250 sec

FREM, ENTERING THE TYNE

The fishing boat on left of picture, returning to the fish quay, is *Frem* (GY 325; see pages 32-33). Entering the Tyne at the same time is cargo ship *Atheras* which was launched in 1966 (20 January), built in Germany by Sietas of Neuenfelde, length 74.2 metres and originally named *Wieland* (IMO 6611904).

On Monday, 2 July 1984, as *Frem* returned in poor weather from the Aberdeen Bank via the Northeast Bank, following a six-day fishing trip, the crew came across an incident two miles east of the Tyne. Tim Stone and Colin Bonham (both aged 30) had gone salmon fishing from Blyth in the early morning with coble *Dawn Marie*, but she was swamped around eight o'clock in a northerly gale and heavy seas and her larch rudder snapped. Tim was lost, last seen by Colin swimming for a lifebelt. *Frem* skipper, Nat Herd, spotted Colin in the water waving his arms at a distance of about 200 yards and he turned the boat so his crew could pull him from the water. It was about 2:25 p.m. as the *Frem* sailed for the Tyne and after he had been in the water for six or more hours. Colin had been clinging to an almost empty five-gallon plastic water container ... which kept him afloat. "He was almost done, it's a miracle Nat saw him," recounted *Frem* co-owner and crewman Paul Wenn. Colin spent the night in Tynemouth Infirmary. His condition was described as "fine" the next day and he was allowed home to East Howdon – so he promptly went to thank Nat Herd of Knott's Flats, Tynemouth, for his rescue. Tim was originally from Cullercoats. "It was a sad incident," fisherman Paul Wenn told the author. He also said, "I am glad they are doing a memorial at the quay. There have been a lot of fishermen lost from here and they can soon be forgotten."

Sailing into the Tyne, 25 September 1987 : (Photo Ref 162-31) Tamron 300 mm lens; Kodak TMAX-400; f/5.6; 1/250 sec

WHITE WINGS (LH 42)

Fishing vessel *White Wings* (LH 42) was built in 1984 at Eyemouth of length 64 feet and with a gross tonnage of 57. The name reminds the author / photographer of winter gulls which visit the river Tyne from the arctic, also known as white-winged gulls, later prompting the name of his publishing company 'White Wings Publishing'. She was photographed at North Shields in 1985.

North Shields fish quay, 27 April 1985 : (Photo Ref 97-19) Kodak Elite 400; f/11; 1/125 sec (hull with name) :
(Photo Ref 97-21) Kodak Elite 400; f/16; 1/250 sec (lifebelt)

PROTECTION JETTY WITH LIFEBELT

The flag pole (its flaking white-painted base is shown here) at the end of the protection (or projection) jetty was cut down some years ago ... and went along with its old lifebelt. AED is Albert Edward Dock (now Royal Quays Marina), just upriver and built in the period 1872-84 for the Tyne Improvement Commission. Royal Quays Marina first opened in late 1998, but opened fully for their first season in 1999. PTA is Port of Tyne Authority which was constituted on 28 June 1968 when the Tyne Improvement Commission (established in 1850) was dissolved on 31 July 1968. The lifebelt in the photograph must have been originally based at Albert Edward Dock and had received a new lease of life at the fish quay.

North Shields fish quay, 27 September 1987 : (Photo Ref 160-19) Kodak Elite 100; f/22; 1/30 sec

KERRY ANN B (SN 168)

Coble *Kerry Ann B* (SN 168) was owned and fished at this time by Alan Dobson ('Dobba'); his mate and assistant for three years (Stephen Thompson) is seen steering her in this photograph. Behind the coble, on the quayside, is a storage area for wooden fish boxes and the pump room (with blue door and window frames) which took saltwater from the river to clean the market and quays. Les Boulton (page 89) has worked on the fish quay since 1968, becoming a quaymaster in 1993 after 25 years with Lilburn's. His first job as quaymaster involved hosing down the quay and market; at first the hose was too wide and needed replacement by one with a narrower bore. Lilburn's dealt with many species of fish, but had been the biggest seller of salmon at North Shields – selling to Leeds, Manchester and London.

North Shields fish quay, 16 January 1988 : (Photo Ref 161-04) Kodak Elite 200; f/8 ½; 1/125 sec

Regulus (BK 79)

Newly painted *Regulus* (Berwick registered ... BK 79) rests out of the water at the Western Quay of North Shields fish quay on 16 January 1988, close to the RNMDSF (Fishermen's Mission) building. The Old High Light (constructed in 1727) is visible on the bank top. *Regulus* was built in 1969 at just under 12 metres in length with a 120 hp main diesel engine. She was built on the south coast of England and operated from Ramsgate (Kent) where she was previously registered. Made of clinker construction with an aft wheelhouse, she was specially built so she could be hauled up onto the beach on a daily basis. Cliff Brand (North Shields) bought her from a Seahouses fishing family in the late 1970s or early 1980s. She was brought to North Shields and first worked on gill nets and later rigged for prawn trawling. Cliff sold her to new owners (Bill Anderson) in Berwick and last saw her there in 1995; she is thought to be still fishing.

North Shields fish quay, 16 January 1988 : (Photo Ref 161-08) Kodak Elite 200; f/8 ½; 1/125 sec

DOROTHY D AND DIVER

The net of fishing vessel *Dorothy D* (ME 45) had become stuck the previous night at 4 pm, one hour from land; she was towed back to harbour. The net, entangled in the boat's propeller, was being freed by a diver. *Dorothy D* was built (1957) in Fraserburgh of length 43 feet and with a gross tonnage of 22. At the time of the photograph the vessel was owned by Robert ('Bob') Paterson of Whitley Bay. For another photograph of *Dorothy D* see opposite the Contents page.

North Shields fish quay, 16 January 1988 :
(Photo Ref 161-23) Kodak Elite 200

Security man (John Ferguson)

John Ferguson was a trawler-man, fishing from North Shields; when he retired he became a security officer at the fish quay for the North Shields Fisherman's Association. He lived in South Shields and Martin Ponton (of William Wight Ltd. the grocers) recalled he was a quiet and lovely man. In the picture John looks out from his security hut at the entrance to the fish quay. John's father's brother worked as a labourer for Smart's on the fish quay. Smart's (based upstairs, where the current RMNDSF office is located) auctioned and sold crabs, lobsters and salmon from four to six large white tables in the area over the road from the New Low Light where there is now a brick wall. At that time there were three markets on the fish quay: a wet fish market; a herring market; and a market for shellfish, crabs, lobsters and salmon. In the morning crabs would be landed to the crab market. Fish merchant John Ellis recalled that the fish quay people used to be very superstitious and if a trawler-man caught a redfish (for example salmon) amongst his normal whitefish net catch, then he would throw the redfish overboard because it was thought bad to mix the two i.e. red and white fish.

When based at the fish quay, John would come aboard Jacky Weatherstone's boat *Karen Obbekaer* and help land her catch. John and 'Big Joe' (Joe 'Acker' Atkinson? who was also from the south side of the Tyne) would receive up to four or five boxes of skate from Jacky and they would take this away, skin the fish and sell them.

North Shields fish quay, 16 January 1988 : (Photo Ref 161-25) Kodak Elite 200; f/8; 1/60 sec

BARRA HEAD

Barra Head was completed in June 1980 (Miho Zosensho, Shimizu), of 4,691 gross tonnage and 363 feet in length, for Salvesen and sold in 1989 to Norwegian owners. Seen here (registered in Leith) sailing up the Tyne, photographed from the fish quay with North and South Shields in the background. The ship shows the distinctive red, white and blue-topped funnel of Salvesen. She had two sister ships: *Sumburgh Head* (built 1977) and *Rora Head* (1980), and all three were in the Salvesen fleet for whom they delivered coal supplies to Central Electricity

Generating Board (CEGB) power stations. Christian Salvesen & Co was established in 1872, based in Leith, and ran whaling ships, colliers, bulk carriers, a liner service to Norway, fishing vessels and oil industry vessels in drilling and support. There is an interesting family history prior to 1872 which is introduced in Somner (1984). In 1989 Salvesen withdrew from shipping to concentrate on their other trading activities. In December 2007 it became a wholly owned subsidiary of French-listed transport group Norbert Dentressangle.

North Shields fish quay, 16 January 1988 : (Photo Ref 161-29) Kodak Elite 200; f/16; 1/250 sec

Rusty aircraft wing / tail fin

The photograph shows an aircraft part trawled up from the North Sea by one of the fishing boats (thought to be the *Mimosa* SN 23) and landed at the fish quay. The item may be from a wing, tail section or rudder. It lies on the quayside near some otter boards and fishing net and is several feet long and wide. It has not been possible to identify to which aircraft collection the part (most likely a wing) went. If any reader has more information – then please contact the author.

At the time of the photograph if a fishing boat caught such an item, or any unexploded ordnance, then a form ('mine claim') could be collected from the Ministry of Agriculture, Fisheries and Food (MAFF) for completion. The form would go to the Navy to decide what to do with a particular item. The boat skipper may be reimbursed

for damage to his fishing gear. MAFF was superseded by DEFRA (Department for the Environment, Food and Rural Affairs) in 2002. Nowadays, such a 'mine claim' form would come from the MMO (Marine Management Organisation), a DEFRA branch created in 2009 and responsible for marine activities in the seas around England and Wales. At the time when both aircraft parts were trawled up (see also page 13) Bill Bridge worked from an office at North Shields for MAFF, but he could not recall the items when the author spoke with him in August 2016. Bill was the MAFF district inspector for thirty years, from 1964, following a period as a fisherman and skipper from Lowestoft where he began on a steam herring drifter. His northeast district covered the coast from Berwick down to Hartlepool and into Yorkshire.

North Shields fish quay, 13 February 1988 : (Photo Ref 162-02) Kodak Elite 400; f/3.8; 1/30 sec

BREKKE'S PAINTERS

Two painters are recorded in the photographs improving the exterior of Brekke's.

Brekke's processing factory (now demolished) stood beside Fish Quay Sands; here fish and prawns were processed for the food industry; their prawns went to France and Spain. A retired fisherman told the author that one of the fish species processed there, for several years, was mock halibut (Greenland halibut) from Iceland. A report (North Tyneside Council 1988) states '... several local processing firms are investing heavily to exploit new markets for fish. Examples include Brekkes who have recently invested about £100,000 in new plant, internal and external alterations, and have now set up links exporting salt cod to Italy.' The general manager was called Joe Norman and the floor manager was Harry Jackson. Joe Norman's son, Alastair, took over as general manager when his father retired.

In later years, following demolition of the factory near Lloyds jetty, improvements to the derelict site saw the creation of a raised promenade and grassed area. The raised promenade links to the Low Lights car park and footpath to Tynemouth. This improvement work (during 2005-2006) incurred a capital cost of £632,000 (funded by North Tyneside Council).

Prior to using the site beside Lloyds jetty, Brekke's was based in the current Caley's building on Tanners Bank, which had previously been used by the Hastie trawlers. When this site was owned by the Hastie trawler men the building was wooden and it finally burnt down. It was rebuilt, in its current form, with little wood

in its composition. Then the later factory was built, beside Fish Quay Sands, in 1964 for the Ranger Fishing Company who owned the very advanced Ranger boats in the 1960s, for example *Ranger Apollo*. The large, steel Ranger fishing boats carried a crew who would fillet and clean their catch and pack them into boxes to store in on-board freezers – a new innovation at the time. A sister ship of the *Ranger Apollo* was the *Gaul* (initially named *Ranger Castor*) – which sank off the coast of Russia (1974) when all thirty six hands were lost. Brekke's took the factory over from the Ranger Fishing Company.

Retired North Shields fisherman Jacky Weatherstone recalled that before the Ranger factory was built in 1964 the land there acted as a boat yard for cobles. He mentioned there was a wooden slope down to the sands and a large post at the top of the slope which served to assist in pulling cobles up from the beach. Retired Tynemouth lifeboat man Trevor Fryer noted that a mortuary once stood on the exact footprint that became the main office in the 1964 factory later taken over by Brekke's.

North Shields fish quay, 16 January 1988 : Page 58: (Photo Ref 161-31) Kodak Elite 200; f/8; 1/125 sec
Page 59: (Photo Ref 161-32) Kodak Elite 200; f/5.6 ½; 1/125 sec

Sarah (LH 183) in Gut

Sarah (LH 183) lies in the Gut at North Shields fish quay, 21 February 1988; behind her are Shonmora and Braw Lads. Sarah was built in 1959 in Denmark of length 55 feet and owned by James and Doreen Hill of Cullercoats. Mr & Mrs Hill also owned Sarah Fish, a merchant who handled a huge amount of prawns; Doreen was secretary for the North Shields Fisherman's Association. Sarah was a Caley Fisheries boat; she underwent a major refit and restoration work during 1998 and then James Hill ran her under 'Shearwater Cruises'. At that time she offered home cooking in a boat retaining most of her original features, during cruises up to six days from the Tyne or the west of Scotland (Oban).

North Shields fish quay, 21 February 1988 : (Photo Ref 162-23) Kodak Elite 400; f/22; 1/250 sec

SECURITY HUT,
LOW LIGHT, BOXES

The blue wooden fish quay security hut (see page 55 with John Ferguson), New Low Light and lots of wooden fish boxes ready for use.

North Shields fish quay, 21 February 1988 : (Photo Ref 162-14) Pentax K 1000; Kodak Elite 400; f/16 ½; 1/250 sec

Prow of *Dorothy May B* (SD 236) (previously *Margaret Weston*)

The foredeck and bow of attractive coble *Dorothy May B* (SD 236) at the fish quay. Built in 1966(?) by J & J Harrisons (of Amble; now called Amble Boat Company) of length 36 feet and six inches; she is no longer based at North Shields. Previously, before her small wheelhouse was added, she was called *Margaret Weston* (SD 236) and had been built as a 'half-decker' for the Weston family of Sunderland. She was then sold to Alan Dobson who fished her from North Shields, gill-netting for cod. Alan sold her to Frank Taylor (current RNLI lifeboat operations manager at Cullercoats) who renamed her *Dorothy May B* since he already had a coble called *Dorothy May* (SN 14). Further changes of ownership have brought such names as *Jenny Louise*, *Chelsea Lee* and *Audrey William*.

North Shields fish quay, 12 June 1988 : (Photo Ref 168-17) Kodak Elite 200; f/16; 1/250 sec

Kalisto (BF 555)

Fishing boat *Kalisto* (BF 555) seen here tied up in the Gut at North Shields fish quay on 12 June 1988. She was built in 1981 and her home port is Aberdeen [according to The United Kingdom fishing vessel list (excluding islands) as at 1st April 2014, Source: Marine Management Organisation Statistics and Analysis Team].

North Shields fish quay, 12 June 1988 :
(Photo Ref 168-09) Kodak Elite 200

ICE CREAM VAN AND NEW HIGH LIGHT

The Western Quay, at North Shields fish quay, has been a regular beat for ice cream vans over many years. Here a van from Jenny's Ices trades below the New High Light on 12 June 1988.

(Photo Ref 169-02) Kodachrome 64; f/11; 1/125 sec

Fireworks, Fish Quay Festival

Evening fireworks at North Shields fish quay (Saturday, 27 May 1989) during the third Fish Quay Festival. This festival, which cost £120,000 to organise, was held over the three days of the Bank Holiday weekend and reported to have attracted at least 600,000 people who spent an estimated one million pounds. Musical acts ranged from Hungarian folk groups to Alan Price (who was educated at Jarrow Grammar School, South Tyneside). The fireworks were orchestrated by Alan Hillary (based in County Durham).

North Shields fish quay, 27 May 1989 : (Photo Ref 169-07) Kodachrome 64; f/8 to f/11; 4 to 8 seconds

LIFEBOAT – FISH QUAY FESTIVAL

Tynemouth all-weather lifeboat *RNLB George and Olive Turner* (52-13) sails amongst the bunting of the Fish Quay Festival. These annual festivals were held at the fish quay between 1987 and 2005. The *RNLB George and Olive Turner* served from the Tyne between 1980 and 1999 under volunteer coxswains John Hogg (coxswain: 1976 – 1986) and Martin Kenny (coxswain: 1986 – 2002).

North Shields fish quay, 28 May 1989 : (Photo Ref 169-36) Kodachrome 64; f/11; 1/125 sec
Portrait: Martin Kenny, North Shields fish quay, 9 July 2016 : (Photo Ref 6676) EOS 30D; EFS 17-85 mm lens; focal length 64 mm; f/13; 1/200 sec; ISO-400

BRIAR (BF 382) INCOMING WITH SN 82

Fishing boats *Briar* (BF 382) and SN 82 (name unknown; registered in North Shields) returning to the Tyne after a day of fishing. *Briar* was built in 1939 at Peterhead of length 39 feet and a gross tonnage of 16. She was owned by John Shiel, a Northumberland lad and welder by trade who owns Sleekburn Welding (Bedlington) and now does work aboard the North Shields boats and with Caley Fisheries. *Briar* was a Caley Fisheries boat.

North Shields fish quay, 13 October 1990 : (Photo Ref 189-30); 300 mm Tamron lens; Kodak Elite 200; f/11 ½; 1/250 sec

GUT VIEW AND FISH MOSAICS

River view from above the fish quay – the fish sculpture and mosaics (foreground), implemented by FreeForm Arts, were installed in 1987. The New Low Light and attached house later became a private residence of the Morse family. Blue-hulled fishing boat *Tudor Time* (SN 21) sits to right of centre in the Gut. She was built in 1957 at Seahouses with length 39 feet and owned (in 1987) by Charles E Armstrong (of North Shields) and Martha A & Ralph Fleming (of East Howdon).

North Shields fish quay, 6 March 1993 : (Photo Ref 204-28) Kodak Elite 100; f/16; 1/125 sec

HEDWIN DEPARTING

Looking upriver from North Shields against the light; work horse *Hedwin* sails downriver, likely with a full load to dump at sea, 6 March 1993. She was the river's resident dredger for 42 years (1969 – 2011) and cleared silt flowing down and deposited from the hills of the North and South Tyne and sand washed in by the tide from the sea (Chaplin & Tiernan 2010). The undulations in the foreground are part of the Naters Bank Fishscape (installed in 1987).

North Shields, 6 March 1993 : (Photo Ref 204-34) Kodak Elite 100; f/16; 1/250 sec

John William (Jackie) Dowse

Retired fisherman John William (Jackie) Dowse (1926 – 2000) views the river mouth from above the fish quay where he lived in Trinity Buildings. Jackie was a North Shields fishing boat owner and fisherman and one of the boats he co-owned was *Condowan* (KY 247). He also owned a coble called *Ocean Pride* (SN 139). The other owners of the *Condowan* were the Morse family fishing brothers Alan and Norman (Norrie). Her name came from the union of: 'Con' from names of boats owned by the Morse family (for example *Congener* and *Conmoran*); 'Dow' from Jackie's surname, and the initial letters ('A' and 'N') from the Christian names of these two Morse brothers. Jackie started his fishing life from Hull on a trawler sailing to the White Sea. He died in 2000 aged 73.

The lifeboat house may be seen with blue shuttering in central distance. This was demolished in 1997. The taller building to the left, with black slate roof, is the Old Low Light, opened as a Heritage Centre in March 2015. Behind Jackie a cluster of dark, slanting rooftops is visible – fish quay smoke houses. Above the smoke house roofs are Lord Collingwood's monument and the white-painted Watch House of Tynemouth Volunteer Life Brigade. The blue and white painted and windowed offices inside the fish quay enclosure, visible at the base of the white New Low Light (but with a road and fence between them), were the quaymaster offices.

North Shields fish quay, 6 March 1993 : (Photo Ref 204-36) Kodak Elite 100; f/16; 1/125 sec

'PIRATE' AND ESTUARY VIEW

One of the fish quay dogs roams beside the Low Lights car park overlooking the Tyne estuary. This dog was called 'Pirate' and was reportedly brought up to North Shields from Grimsby by his owner, Alec Mussell. Alec had a brother, Geordie, and both were Grimsby skippers who came to North Shields for the better fishing – coming for sprats. Pirate was then kept and looked after by Rouble and Meggie Chicken, owners at the Low Lights Tavern on Brewhouse Bank. He roamed the fish quay for many years and was thought to have fathered many offspring. "He was a stud!" fisherman Mark Dean told the author, with fond memories.

Another fisherman thought Pirate had been brought from Grimsby by 'Canadian' Barry, but the report above appears more correct.

North Shields fish quay, 31 January 1993 : (Photo Ref 204-04) Pentax K 1000; 38-140 mm lens; Kodak Elite 100; f/8 ½; 1/125 sec

TALL SHIPS – *ASGARD II*

The river Tyne first hosted a Tall Ships' Race in summer 1986. These annual races, held since 1956, were for sailing ships and to encourage international friendship through sail training. The rules insist that over half of each ship's crew must comprise young people aged 15 to 25.

Tynemouth photographer Mr J. Neil Fletcher, who ran a shop and studio and normally sold 200 rolls of film a week, had sold 2,500 by Saturday lunchtime (19 July) according to the North Shields News Guardian of 25 July 1986.

Brigantine *Asgard II* was commissioned on 7 March 1981 and built as a sail training vessel in Arklow, County Wicklow. She was the Irish national sail training vessel until she sank in the Bay of Biscay in 2008 when sailing for maintenance in La Rochelle. Plans to raise the vessel in 2009 were not followed through and she was left resting on the sandy sea bottom. It is thought her sinking was due to a collision with a submerged object, the crew abandoned her as she took on water. Some artefacts including the vessel's bell were recovered in 2010 by a team of Irish divers. Plans were unveiled in 2015 for a replacement tall ship with twice the capacity of *Asgard II*.

Asgard II, leaving the Tyne, 19 July 1986 :
(Photo Ref 154-07) Kodak Tri-X

TALL SHIPS – *ALEXANDER VON HUMBOLDT*

The German barque *Alexander von Humboldt* approaches the Tyne entrance to leave on the Tall Ships' Race (1993) to Bergen on the west coast of Norway. This ship was originally built in 1906 at Bremen as a lightship and operated in the North and Baltic Seas until retirement in 1986 to be next converted to a three-masted barque and re-launched in 1988; she had 25 sails. Traffic caused problems with many roads closed during the week as folk flocked on Tyneside to see the great ships. The first of the tall ships to reach Bergen was *Aurora*, a Russian ship, on the morning of Wednesday 21 July. This was the second time the Tyne hosted the Cutty Sark Tall Ships' Race.

Tyne river mouth, 17 July 1993 : (Photo Ref 223-03) Pentax K 1000; Kodak Elite 100

'Coal diggers on the Black Middens' (1921) Watercolour

An evocative painting by North Shields artist Victor Noble Rainbird (see also page viii). Bare boulder clay cliffs overlooked the Black Middens (see also page 76) until landscaping during the 1970s (- 1980s) softened their outline into the modern banksides with footpaths and promenade we see today. The tide is out a little and has uncovered rocks at the cliff base where people may be seen at work collecting sea-washed coal from the shore and perhaps loading it into the two small wooden boats with oars. The man in foreground, with white shirt, appears to be carrying a bag with coal over his shoulder. Rainbird had such a deft use of brush and paint to conjure convincing human forms from just a few carefully placed strokes with muted colour. The sky is grey with cloud cover, perhaps depicting quite a typical day for such a scene in the cooler months. The coal gatherers were likely very local Tyne folk with little money, collecting fuel to warm their homes. For more information on the artist refer to www.victornoblerainbird.com.

Image and permission to use were kindly provided courtesy of Dave Young.
Photograph by Alison Spedding Photography (www.alisonspedding.co.uk)

PART TWO

RIVER TYNE
1991 AND 2007 – 2016
A BIT MORE MODERN ... AND A FEW BIRDS

The author has a keen interest in the birds of the lower Tyne

Cameras	Fujica ST 705	Single Lens Reflex (SLR), 35 mm film camera
	Canon EOS 30D	Single Lens Reflex, digital camera
	Canon EOS 7D Mk II	Single Lens Reflex, digital camera
Lenses	Tamron 300 mm, manual	f/5.6
	Canon EFS 17-85 mm	f/4-5.6 IS USM
	Canon EF 70-200 mm	f/4 L USM
	Canon EF 1.4x II extender	
Photographic film	Kodak T-Max 400	35 mm, black and white negative, 400 ASA/ISO

Feather from a curlew: a bird which feeds on the rocks, sand and mud of the Tyne.

BLACK MIDDENS

Text from the reverse of the author's Tyne River Mouth notecard featuring this image:

THE BLACK MIDDENS
The sun's rays burst from the southeast behind the November morning
clouds overlooking the Tyne estuary (northeast England).
Towards the centre and foreground rest the Black Middens
rocky shore, to be sea-covered at high tide – a notorious maritime hazard
of times past and modern. The Tyne south pier stretches beyond
with Souter lighthouse (National Trust) in the distance on the right.

Text from the author's personal journal entry of 16 March 2015:

One of his [i.e. Fred Crowell, a restorer and repairer of boats] facts was about the naming of the Black Middens rocky outcrop on the north side of the Tyne mouth. He said the name Midden stems from the fact that rubbish was dumped there at one time, before the piers were built, when the deposits would be washed away by the incoming tides. The 'Black', he told us, originated from the fact that a coal seam was exposed here on the shore and people came to dig out the coal at low tide.

Black Midden Rocks at the mouth of the river Tyne, 11 November 2007 : (Photo Ref 6165) EOS 30D; EFS 17-85 mm lens; focal length 53 mm; f/14; 1/500 sec; ISO-400

DFDS FERRY

DFDS Seaways cruise ferry *Princess Seaways* arriving on the Tyne just after nine o'clock on the morning of Sunday, 25 March 2012, passing the North Shields river-ferry landing stage. The two cruise ferries *King Seaways* and *Princess Seaways* ply their route between the river Tyne and the Netherlands where they berth at Ijmuiden, near Amsterdam. A ferry arrives daily on the Tyne in the morning and another leaves for Holland in the late afternoon, with overnight crossings. DFDS Seaways was named as the world's best ferry operator each year from 2011 to 2015. *Princess Seaways* was built in 1986, has a crew of 140 and can carry over 1,200 guests and 600 cars; she has a cruising speed of 21 knots and is of length 163 metres. Following behind is Cullercoats B class lifeboat *Hylton Burdon* (B-811) on exercise.

Steaming upriver, 25 March 2012 : (Photo Ref 8351) EOS 30D; EFS 17-85 mm lens; focal length 85 mm; f/14; 1/500 sec; ISO-400

DENNIS CLARK

At the far end of the extension (or protection) jetty fisherman Dennis (Ned) Clark is shown working on a salmon net with a small knife. This quite new net had only lasted a few weeks the previous summer – it was of poor quality and any salmon that were caught had been able to break the net with their strength and so escape. Therefore Dennis was cutting off the lower, weighted, lead line and top cork float line to use on a new net; he would discard the old one. He told the author he would not be fishing for salmon during summer 2016, but his son Peter would, as usual. One of the Clark family cobles used for salmon is called *Silver Coquet* (SN 8); she was built at Amble in 1960 by J & J Harrison. Currently the salmon fishing season takes place over the three summer months of June, July and August from Monday to Friday. Dennis has spent his working life fishing from the Tyne and is regional representative of the National Federation of Fishermen's Organisations (NFFO); his father Douglas Clark (born 1923) is a retired northeast fisherman (Turner 2014).

North Shields fish quay, 17 April 2016 : (Photo Ref 5034) EOS 30D; EFS 17-85 mm lens; focal length 38 mm; f/13; 1/100 sec; ISO-400

QE2

The Cunard liner *Queen Elizabeth 2* (registered in Southampton) sailed onto the Tyne on Sunday evening, 16 September 2007 – for a brief visit of a night and a day. This was her first visit to the Tyne and took place during the ship's fortieth anniversary celebrations – on a voyage around the British Isles. She berthed at Tyne Commission Quay where her captain, Ian McNaught, renamed it Northumbrian Quay. She is seen here on her departure from the Tyne, passing the fish quay on Monday's wet evening with droplets of rain blurring light passing through the camera lens. The Scottish fishing vessel to left of picture is *Provider*. The *QE2* was due to return to the Tyne on 8-9 October 2008 before her retirement to Dubai into life as a hotel, but her final guise as a hotel has been stalled due to financial considerations.

North Shields fish quay, 17 September 2007 : (Photo Ref 5560) EOS 30D; EFS 17-85 mm lens; focal length 17 mm; f/11; 1/30 sec; ISO-400

McNulty Kittiwakes

Black-legged kittiwakes *Rissa tridactyla* have been recorded nesting on buildings and man-made structures along the river Tyne since 1949. This photograph shows a family at the McNulty Offshore yard, South Shields, on 10 July 2009. Kittiwakes were recorded nesting at the McNulty yard, on the engineering workshop, between 1997 and 2014 in which year there were 52 apparently occupied nests producing 50 young. It is likely this building will be demolished (it is in a poor state of repair) now that the yard has been sold to the Port of Tyne and the quayside is under major renovation. Nesting kittiwakes along the Tyne continue to increase in number, with a record 1,011 nests in 2015 topped by 1,074 nests in summer 2016 (detail from surveys by, and records of, author D M Turner). Kittiwakes are decreasing nationally and the species has been added to the red list of bird species of conservation concern … having shown a severe decline in its breeding population over the recent 25 years and more (Eaton, et. al. 2015).

Tyne kittiwake family, 10 July 2009 : (Photo Ref 1976) EOS 30D; EF 70-200 mm lens with EF 1.4x extender; focal length 280 mm; f/9; 1/500 sec; ISO-320

SABINE'S GULL WITH RIVER VIEW

An immature Sabine's gull *Xema sabini* can be seen here in flight over the river Tyne with the cranes of Tyne Dock (South Shields) in the distance and a type of tug boat on the river (showing two diffused amber lights). This was a rare visiting bird to the Tyne which spent from 25 October 2009 (when the author first found it) to 9 November 2009 frequenting the river mouth. It was observed and photographed by many local and visiting folk with an interest in ornithology. Quite often it would call quietly as it patrolled up and down North Shields fish quay; it had distinctive wing markings and a slightly forked tail. This species nests in the arctic; Canadian and Greenland birds cross the north Atlantic and some descend our coastline on their way to winter off southwest Africa.

Beside North Shields fish quay, 3 November 2009 : (Photo Ref 4248) EOS 30D; EF 70-200 mm lens;
focal length 200 mm; f/4.5; 1/160 sec; ISO-1600

TOMMY BAILEY (SENIOR)

Fisherman Tommy Bailey (senior) stands aboard his coble *Royal Sovereign* (SN 356) in the Gut at North Shields fish quay. He is surrounded by his large crab and lobster pots to catch shellfish offshore. A fisherman from the age of fifteen, he started aboard his father's new fishing boat *Girl Irene* (SN 19), built in Banff in 1957. From 1960-62 he spent two years as a deckhand on *Condowan* (KY 247) under skipper Jackie Dowse (see page 70). He next served on Richard Irvin trawlers, and more, before gaining his skipper's ticket in 1975. His story is explained in more detail in Turner (2014); he retired as a fisherman in 2010.

North Shields fish quay, 3 May 2009 : (Photo Ref 1339) EOS 30D; EFS 17-85 mm lens; focal length 28 mm; f/10; 1/160 sec; ISO-400

Guy Laurence

Filipino fisherman Guy Laurence is shown net mending at the fish quay. Guy was one of a crew of four Filipino men plus a Whitby skipper – fishing with Whitby registered vessel *Success III* (WY 212). The crew were preparing for another 6-7 day North Sea fishing trip, landing their catches at Scarborough and in Denmark. They were fishing the 'tail end' of the prawn season, catching a few fish also and had caught a large shark the previous week – quickly released alive back into the sea. Guy had been with the trawler for two years and was to return home at the end of the year, probably to come back early in 2013. The author saw and photographed Guy, mending nets again, at North Shields fish quay on 23 February 2014, while he was still working in the North Sea aboard *Success III*.

North Shields fish quay, 22 April 2012 : (Photo Ref 8878) EOS 30D; EFS 17-85 mm lens; focal length 20 mm; f/15; 1/500 sec; ISO-400

HERRING GULL WITH FISH

The herring gull *Larus argentatus* must be the most common and regular bird of the Tyne river mouth. Here a bird in its first year flies up from the river water in the Gut at the fish quay – it has picked up fish remains from one of the boats sorting their catch ... flying away for a feast.

North Shields fish quay, 11 December 1991 : (Photo Ref 204-29) Fujica ST 705; Tamron 300 mm lens;
Kodak T-Max 400; f/11; 1/500 sec; ISO-400

ICELAND GULL

The Iceland gull *Larus glaucoides* is a pale, moderate-sized gull from the arctic which may be found, in small numbers, each winter on the river Tyne. The individual in the photograph is a bird in its first-winter plumage, showing neat and fine barring on the undertail-coverts; there is no black in the wing feathers and the main plumage tone is a soft brownish-grey or buff. In the second year their plumage becomes whiter and blotchy in appearance before developing pearl-grey wing and mantle colouration as they mature. The eyes of a first-year bird are dark; when they become adult the iris is pale yellow and the bill shows a greenish-yellow hue. In the winter of 1996-97 there were considered to be 9-11 Iceland gulls in Northumberland which included at least four birds visiting the North Shields fish quay and Tyne estuary area (Turner, in: Day & Hodgson 2003). In the winter period of 2007-08, 4-6 birds of this species were recorded in Northumberland (Turner, in: Dean, et. al. 2015); North Shields fish quay remains a favoured locality for this species.

North Shields fish quay, 27 December 2008 : (Photo Ref 0113) EOS 30D; EF 70-200 mm lens with EF 1.4x extender; focal length 280 mm; f/6.3; 1/320 sec; ISO-400

KEITH HARVEY
(RETIRED FISHERMAN)

Retired fisherman Keith Harvey is pictured outside the New Dolphin public house at the fish quay with his dog Sasha, awaiting opening time. Keith told the author that Sasha was twelve at this time. She died in early 2016. Sasha was a Staffie (Staffordshire Bull Terrier) / whippet cross of whom Keith reported she was ... "like greased lightning, her, when she was young!" He would exercise her on the Fish Quay Sands and she was able to keep pace with two greyhounds which also ran there. The New Dolphin pub, opposite the Richard Irvin Building, changed ownership in summer 2013 and is now the Staith House.

North Shields fish quay, 15 August 2010 :
(Photo Ref 7666) EOS 30D; EFS 17-85 mm lens;
focal length 22 mm; f/16;
1/40 sec; ISO-400

Keith Harvey (continued)

Keith fished on most of the North Shields boats of the time, but did not enjoy one-day trips fishing for prawns – he preferred longer trips of several days. He said, "I was nearly always on the Scots boats, Scotsmen, seine net boats." Those he served with included *Clonmore*, *Lothian Rose*, *Fisher Rose* and *Ocean Venture*. Davy Boyter was skipper of *Clonmore* on five- to six-day trips catching all sorts of fish species out of Whitby and Aberdeen ... Keith was a crew member with her for twelve years. He also fished on the *Helga Risager* from North Shields. When aged 15 he got his first job on the fish quay, as a store boy for Ronnie Longstaff ... sorting out fish. Later he joined the Merchant Navy before becoming a fisherman.

A friend of Keith, called Eric Luke ('Lukey') first started on the fish quay as a store boy, like Keith. Then he became a fish filleter for Dennis Bell who played for Sunderland. "He was a good footballer," reported Eric who then became a fish porter for Caley Fisheries, at the fish quay, a job he held for about 23 years.

Portrait: North Shields fish quay,
20 June 2016 : (Photo Ref 6303) EOS 30D;
EFS 17-85 mm lens; focal length 59 mm;
f/10; 1/50 sec; ISO-400

TERRY REED (CALEY'S AUCTIONEER)

After working for Purdy's (where he started in 1972) as factory office manager Terry Reed (see notes on page 13) went to work for Richard Irvin & Sons from 1976 until 1988, then was poached by Caley Fisheries and worked for them until his retirement on 29 January 2016 (aged 65). While working at Purdy's the company made fish cakes, fish fingers and frozen battered fish portions which were distributed to Cornwall and all over the country. The fish portions came from the Ranger boats and were frozen aboard ... high quality fish; Purdy's and the Ranger boats were part of the same company. In the photograph Terry, with yellow top, is checking the fish on the market before the morning sales commenced – when he would auction the fish. To the front of Terry is another Caley's auctioneer (Steve Smith) and behind, in the distance, is local fish merchant Paul Lin.

North Shields fish quay market, 3 December 2012 : (Photo Ref 3475) EOS 30D; EFS 17-85 mm lens; focal length 17 mm; f/4; 1/30 sec; ISO-1000

LES BOULTON (QUAYMASTER)

Les Boulton (page 52) has worked on the fish quay since 1968, becoming a quaymaster in 1993 after 25 years with Lilburn's. His first job with Lilburn's was with a filleting machine after which he went on to hand filleting on a bench. Then he became a fish buyer on the fish quay market. Lilburn's dealt with all species of fish … such as cod, haddock, monk, etc. In the main photograph Les is recorded hosing the fish quay in front of the windowed quaymasters' office and overlooking the Tyne. The portrait photograph shows Les in the morning beside the Gut and with the Old High Light (built 1727) above on the bankside next to the houses of Trinity Buildings.

North Shields fish quay, hosing down, 9 November 2008 : (Photo Ref 9866) EOS 30D; EFS 17-85 mm lens; focal length 35 mm; f/9; 1/100 sec; ISO-400

North Shields fish quay, portrait of Les, 5 July 2016 : (Photo Ref 6578) EOS 30D; EFS 17-85 mm lens; focal length 68 mm; f/10; 1/100 sec; ISO-400

SUNSET SHOT

Fishing boat *Pilot Star* (B 185), built in 1964, returns to the fish quay on a late, winter afternoon after the sun had set; her wooden, black-painted hull and white shelter deck may be seen as the light fails. She was re-registered, later in 2015, as B 35 (B stands for Belfast) while the author recorded her at North Shields under registration B 85 on 21 August 2016. While on holiday on the west coast of Scotland, the author photographed this vessel in Mallaig harbour on 18 August 2015 as he waited for the Caledonian MacBrayne ferry to Armadale on the Isle of Skye.

North Shields fish quay, 7 February 2015 : (Photo Ref 7568) EOS 30D; EFS 17-85 mm lens; focal length 85 mm; f/9; 1/30 sec; ISO-400

REFERENCES – PRINTED

Armstrong, K. & Dixon, P. 2014 North Tyneside Steam. Northern Voices Community Projects, Whitley Bay.

Chaplin, M. & Tiernan, D. 2010. Tyne People. Port of Tyne, Tyne Dock, South Shields.

Day, J.C. & Hodgson, M.S. 2003. The Atlas of Wintering Birds in Northumbria. Northumberland and Tyneside Bird Club.

Dean, T., Myatt, D., Cadwallender, M. & Cadwallender, T. 2015. Northumbria Bird Atlas. Northumberland and Tyneside Bird Club.

Dodds, G.L. 2013. A short history of North Shields. Albion Press.

Eaton, M., Aebischer, N., Brown, A., Hearn, R., Lock, L., Musgrove, A., Noble, D., Stroud, D. & Gregory, R. 2015. Birds of Conservation Concern 4: the population status of birds in the UK, Channel Islands and Isle of Man. *British Birds* 108: 708-746.

Elliott, J. & Charlton, D. 1994. Backworth: An illustrated history of the mines and railways. Chilton Iron Works, Houghton-le-Spring.

FISH (Folk Interested in Shields Harbour). 2006. North Shields, the New Quay and the fish quay conservation areas: FISHcast Community Character Statement. North Tyneside Council.

Garson, W.S. 1926. The origin of North Shields and its growth. (Later 1992 edition, published by Fish Quay Festival Limited).

Grant, P.J. 1982, 1986. Gulls, a guide to identification. T & A D Poyser Ltd.

Guthrie, J. 1880. The River Tyne: its history and resources. Andrew Reid (Newcastle-upon-Tyne).

Hollerton, E. 1997. Images of England, North Shields. Tempus Publishing Ltd.

Hollerton, E. 2000. Images of England, Around North Shields, the Second Selection. Tempus Publishing Ltd.

Hope, P. 2013. North Shields from old photographs. Amberley Publishing.

Johnson, R.W. Late 1890s. The making of the River Tyne. The Walter Scott Press, Newcastle-on-Tyne.

McKenzie, P. 1983. W.G. Armstrong: The Life and Times of Sir William George Armstrong, Baron Armstrong of Cragside. Longhirst Press.

Mortimer, P. 1987. The last of the hunters: life with the fishermen of North Shields. North Tyneside Libraries & Arts Department.

Muus, B. J. & Dahlstrøm, P. 1974. Collins Guide to the Sea Fishes of Britain and North-Western Europe. Wm Collins Sons and Co Ltd, Glasgow. First published in Denmark in 1964.

Nautilus Consulants. 1990. North Shields Fishery Industry Study: unified management structure and business plan. Prepared for North Tyneside Council by Nautilus Consultants of Elbe Street, Edinburgh.

North Tyneside Council. 1988. The North Sea Fishing Industry. National Conference: 5 October 1988, Park Hotel, Grand Parade, Tynemouth. 'North Shields – A major UK Fishing Port' (Report).

Olsen's Fisherman's Nautical Almanack. 1987. E.T.W. Dennis & Sons Ltd, Scarborough.

Philip's. 2005. Street Atlas: Tyne & Wear.

Side Publications, Newcastle upon Tyne. (1988). North Shields Fish Quay and Fishing Industry, Exhibition pack.

Somner, G. 1984. From 70 North to 70 South: A history of the Christian Salvesen fleet (Christian Salvesen Ltd) ISBN 0-9509199-0-X

Soper, T. & Powell, D. 2008. Wildlife of the North Atlantic. Bradt Travel Guides Ltd.

Turner, D.M. 2010. Counts and breeding success of Black-legged Kittiwakes *Rissa tridactyla* nesting on man-made structures along the River Tyne, northeast England, 1994-2009, *Seabird*, Vol. 23, 111 – 126.

Turner, D.M. 2014. Fish Quay Folk of North Shields. White Wings Publishing.

van der Meljden, L.A. 2002. Klyne Tugs (Lowestoft) Ltd. Lekko International, 133: 3-15; Jan/Feb 2002

Wade, S. 2005. The torso in the tank and other stories; True crimes from around Tyne and Wear. Black and White Publishing Ltd., Edinburgh.

Warn, C.R. 1976. Railways of the Northumberland Coalfield: Rails across Northumberland Part 4. Frank Graham, Newcastle upon Tyne.

Warn, C.R. 1976. Waggonways and Early Railways of Northumberland. Frank Graham, Newcastle upon Tyne.

Wheeler, A. 1978. Key to the Fishes of Northern Europe. Frederick Warne (Publishers) Ltd, London.

Wright, R. 2002. Beyond the piers: A tribute to the fishermen of North Shields. The People's History Ltd., Seaham.

Wright, R. 2003. North Shields: Memories of Fish 'n' Ships. The People's History Ltd., Seaham.

Young, D. 2015. From Dark to Light: Victor Noble Rainbird Exhibition at the Old Low Light North Shields, 10 July – 6 September 2015. Friends of Victor Noble Rainbird.

Newspapers: The Journal (Newcastle), North Shields News Guardian

County Borough of Tynemouth, Proceedings of the Council 1970-71. North Shields Library.

References – online

Greenpeace Media

Wikipedia

www.behindthename.com — some detail on the name Ephraim

www.britishlistedbuildings.co.uk — includes accumulator-tower-in-albert-edward-dock

www.clydesite.co.uk/clydebuilt — detail on *Northumbrian Water* ship

www.conservapedia.com — information on the river Tyne

www.fundamentally.net — Sustainable food (information on halibut)

www.HHTandN.org — Hartlepool History Then and Now (*Golden Ray*)

www.historicalrfa.org — Royal Fleet Auxiliary Historical Society (Re: RFA *Sir Tristram*)

http://iancoombe.tripod.com/index.html — Merchant Navy Nostalgia (+ Christian Salvesen)

www.leithshipyards.com information on *Hedwin* (search for '*Hedwin* tyne' on internet)

www.mjseafood.com

www.nationalnumbers.co.uk/dvla-guide/year-of-issue-149.htm — Vehicle registration letters

www.northtyneside.gov.uk — North Shields fish quay: projects and awards (Brekke's)

www.ntsra.org.uk — North Tyneside Steam Railway Association

www.quaymarinas.com	Includes Royal Quays Marina information
www.shipsnostalgia.com	(includes Loyal Class fleet tenders)
www.shipspotting.com	some detail on *Northumbrian Water* ship
www.thebiggreenpledge.org.uk	(includes detail on the Tyne interceptor sewer)
www.trawlerpictures.net	(includes *Dorothy May B* and South Shields)
www.tynemouth-lifeboat.org	Tynemouth lifeboat station website
www.tynemouthfineart.com	Tynemouth Fine Art, the Linskill Centre
www.tynetugs.co.uk	
www.victornoblerainbird.com	Friends of Victor Noble Rainbird

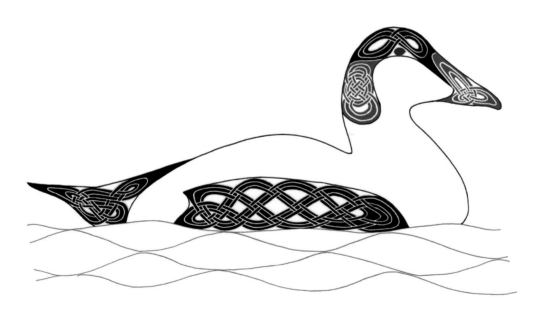

COMMON EIDER

The eider is a large sea duck and we have a regular wintering population in the lower reaches of the River Tyne, up to thirty or so, with smaller summering numbers.

'Cuddy (Male Eider) Duck, original hand drawn design © Cathy McCracken'

ACKNOWLEDGEMENTS

Thanks are extended from the author to ... ...

all his friends and contacts at North Shields fish quay ... for sharing their stories and knowledge. Especially to the quaymasters over many years and fish quay managers ... Jeremy Pritchard and Nik Hanlon, for allowing free access and providing assistance. Also, Tynemouth RNLI lifeboat station staff and volunteers for access, assistance and encouragement.

Discover North Tyneside (North Shields Library) and its staff: Martyn Hurst, Diane Leggett, Joyce Marti and Frances Southwick.

for inclusion of Victor Noble Rainbird paintings: David Hirst (Tynemouth Fine Art), Alison Spedding and Dave Young (Friends of Victor Noble Rainbird).

for help with adjustment of salmon and curlew feather photographs: Graham Relf;

for use of her eider duck design: Cathy McCracken;

for work on the layout and design of the book: Heather Macpherson (Raspberry Creative Type).

for assistance from many individuals with background information and stories: Keith Alexander, Tony Asiamah, Sheena A'violet (J P Knight), Thomas Bailey (senior), Bill Bridge, Bob Brown, Jimmy Brown, Dorothy Brownlee, Les Boulton, Cliff Brand, Stephen Charters, Dennis Clark, Malcolm Cook, Peter Dade, Mark Dean, Andy Dixon (Caley Fisheries), Alan Dobson, Kenneth Downie, Paul Dowse, Tony Dunn (quaymaster), Roy Elliott, John Ellis, Richie Foster, Trevor Fryer, Craig Hall, Keith Harvey, Larry Irvine, Hilla Kay, Martin Kenny, Guy Laurence, Denis Leighton, Richard ('Dicky') Leighton, Paul Lin, Eric ('Lukey') Luke, Mick MacDonald, Stuart Morland (Coble and Keelboat Society), Ray Morse, Barry Moss, Ephraim Fenwick ('Fen') Mundy (junior), Ray Mundy, Geoff Nugent, Martin Ponton, Terry Reed, Ian Riches, Paul Robinson, Matthew Simms, Paul Spivey, James Storey, John Sturmey, George ('Geordie') Sunderland, Brian Telford, Colin Walton, Paul Watson, Jacky Weatherstone, and Paul Wenn.

for assistance from these further resources and organisations: Bamburgh Castle Aviation Museum, Caley Fisheries, Coble and Keelboat Society, Hartlepool library (Reference Department), Keel Row Bookshop, directors and staff of Klyne Tugs (Lowestoft) Limited, Marine Management Organisation (North Shields office), North East Aircraft Museum and the Port of Tyne Harbour Office.

for encouragement with photography over many years: friends and members of Tynemouth Photographic Society, West Chirton / Trinity Church Young Wives group, Northumberland & Tyneside Bird Club, Tynemouth RNLI lifeboat station and supporters, National Trust, Newcastle RSPB group, Natural History Society of Northumbria, Northumberland Wildlife Trust, the Seabird Group, the Old Low Light Heritage Centre (North Shields fish quay), my family and more besides.

the business sponsors for their involvement and encouragement ...

Gold Sponsors   Irvins brasserie, North Shields Fish Quay Company Ltd

Silver Sponsors   J R Fisheries, Percy A Hudson Ltd, Seaview Fisheries

Bronze Sponsor   Royal Quays Marina (Quay Marinas Ltd)

and finally ... for all her encouragement and support in pursuance of this project ... my fiancée, Linda (Katie) Charlton.

... please accept apologies from the author for any accidental omissions and errors.

INDEX TO VESSELS MENTIONED IN THE TEXT

Index to people mentioned in the text

Index to natural life mentioned in the text

Index to other things

NORTH SHIELDS FISH QUAY COMPANY LIMITED

Market Office, Fish Quay, North Shields NE30 1JA   Tel. 0191 257 5422

NSFQ Company is the company behind North Shields Fish Quay,

England's premier North Sea Fishing Port

- 24 Hour berthing
- Deep water berthing
- Large scale ice supply
- Fish market
- Chill storage
- 800 m quay space
- Excellent transport links
- Chandlery, nets & gear
- Fuel & lubricants

SEAVIEW FISHERIES

12 – 14 Union Quay, North Shields,
Tyne and Wear NE30 1HJ
Tel: 0191 296 0642 / 0191 296 2926

Wholesale and retail fish merchants, suppliers to the fish and chip shop trade, restaurants, etc.
We are also a salmon specialist and have our own smokehouse. Established 1987.
We are a small family run business.
We buy fish from various ports including: Hull, Grimsby, Scrabster and Peterhead, but most comes from the North Shields fish quay market.

J R FISHERIES

30-31 Union Quay
Fish Quay
North Shields
Tyne and Wear
NE30 1HJ
Tel. 0191 259 2102
24 hour Answerphone

Wet fish shop and smoke house.

Local and nationwide deliveries.

We skin and bone, fillet, pack, sell and distribute. Our locally sourced fresh fish and shellfish include cod, haddock, salmon, lemon sole, Craster kippers, crab, prawn and mussels.

Come and take a look … we are next to Irvins brasserie and opposite the Staith House.

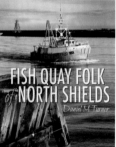